MW01282983

CARE
to LEAD

HOW TO MASTER AND IMPLEMENT FOUR KEYS TO LEADERSHIP:

COMMUNICATION, ACCOUNTABILITY, RELATIONSHIPS AND EXAMPLE OF EXCELLENCE

ALEC MCGALLIARD

ISBN: 978-1-942761-92-1

Cover design and formatting: Archangel Ink

 **Archangel Ink**

Contents

CARE to Lead Bonus Resource

Before you begin reading, I have a free bonus to offer you.

In addition to the information already provided in this book, I have created an introductory video further discussing the CARE Leadership Tools and how they can benefit your organization.

To view your free bonus video, visit my website, mcgalliardconsulting.com.

In addition, the website includes information on how to arrange on-site training for your organization to fully leverage CARE to Lead.

Check it out and connect with me if you have any questions.

- Alec McGalliard

Introduction

I know what you're thinking. It's the same thing I was thinking when my boss asked me (i.e., told me) to read another leadership book: *Please, no, not another leadership book!*

Over the past twenty-seven-plus years in the commercial nuclear industry, I've been "asked" to read *Crucial Conversations, The OZ Principles, Facilitative Leadership, The Situational Leader, The Toyota Way*, and *The Seven Habits of Highly Effective People*, just to name a few. So what makes me think I, a person still trying to become a great leader, need to write another leadership book—especially since I am not a writer, a leadership consultant, or a world-renowned expert in the leadership field?

The short answer—one thing you will notice throughout this book is that I prefer the short answer—is that, while all of the books I mentioned provided valuable tools and insight into what it takes to be a great leader, I have always felt they are just too dadgum long and wordy. And, in some cases, they're not realistic in their day-to-day application.

My other justification for writing this book is that, as a product of the United States Navy Nuclear Submarine Fleet and the commercial nuclear industry, I feel we need one more acronym to remember: CARE.

In truth, CARE
   Communication,
   Accountability,
   Relationships, and
   Example of Excellence

came into being over a long weekend of pondering. I wondered why I sometimes succeeded and sometimes failed as a leader, and what changes I needed to make in my personal performance to become a better leader. As I thought about my role in both my failures and successes, and what worked and didn't work in each situation, one overriding principle came to mind. It was a principle that was consistently reinforced during my childhood: the Golden Rule.

In case you're not familiar with the Golden Rule, it's very simple: "Do unto others as you would have them do unto you." Or, if you prefer the non-biblical version, "Treat others like you want to be treated." I know that sounds simple, but I believe it's a value we need much more of in our professional and personal lives. And once I realized the Golden Rule was the foundation of how I try to conduct myself, I started applying it to my job on a daily basis. The CARE Leadership Tools are a direct result of that.

Personally, I would do almost anything for a leader who consistently practices the Golden Rule and the CARE Leadership Tools.

At this point, I will make a disclaimer about the Golden Rule, as some will say it can't be applied universally in the professional world. You could argue a manager can't apply the rule to the act of terminating someone for performance-related issues or laying someone off as dictated by market/economic decisions.

I would advocate that those situations dictate the required action (termination or layoffs), but the way you *treat people* while dealing with those situations is where you apply the Golden Rule.

I truly believe that Communication, Accountability, Relationships, and Example of Excellence are the cornerstones of true leadership. In this book, I share some simple thoughts that leaders can easily implement on a day-to-day basis that might prevent them from making the same mistakes I made. Along the way, I will share personal stories of success and failure that really paint the picture of how the CARE Leadership Tools can facilitate better leadership.

The CARE Leadership Tools will be beneficial to people in a variety of leadership roles, including first-time and experienced leaders and supervisors, as well as managers and executives that need a little tune-up on some key elements of leadership. *CARE to Lead* is intended to be a quick, commonsense read that can be completed in a couple of hours over a weekend and quickly referenced as situations dictate. There are no required certifications, no surveys or self-tests/assessments to complete—just a new perspective on what has worked and not worked for me over the past twenty-seven years.

As I mentioned earlier, I am not a "certified" leadership expert. Consequently, some might dismiss the CARE Leadership Tools.

However, I contend that a set of tools developed by someone who started at the bottom, worked his way up, and goes to work every day trying to be a better leader offers a different perspective than someone in academia who spent years "studying" leadership. Notice I said different, not right or wrong. The CARE Leadership Tools are meant to complement and work in conjunction with other leadership models. I do not believe any one set of leadership tools addresses all of the issues leaders face, or the many different personalities at our places of employment. However, I do believe that the CARE Leadership Tools provide a solid foundation for working with people of all ages, genders, nationalities, races, etc.

Though CARE is an acronym, it clearly has another meaning. I submit to you that if you don't care about your performance, your job, your coworkers, or your employees, in the traditional sense of the word, you need to seriously consider changing jobs.

A quick note about my writing style. I write like I talk—with clear and concise thoughts explained in my North Carolina/Texas-influenced dialect and with very few big words.

And a final point about this book before we get into

the CARE Leadership Tools: As I was writing this book, I kept asking myself if it was long enough compared to other titles on the subject. Then I thought, who cares? The intent is for you to be able to read it in a couple of hours and refer back to it when needed, not to write a novel or create a textbook with worksheets, surveys, questionnaires, and a bunch of philosophical quotes.

The CARE Leadership Tools are meant to be simple and complement other leadership models and tools.

I invite you to move on to the exploration of the CARE Leadership Tools and then to the life experiences from which they evolved. I promise I will keep it short and sweet. I promise to get to the point.

Part I

The CARE Leadership Tools

CARE Leadership Tools

As you read the CARE Leadership Tools, I hope you'll take the opportunity to reflect on your leadership style, your successes and failures as a leader, and how the CARE tools might influence your approach in the future.

An essential part of applying the CARE Leadership Tools is the ability to be self-critical. You have to be willing to look back on a situation in your professional or personal life and evaluate what was positive and what needs improvement. This is how you apply lessons learned to future situations. And this self-reflection is critical if you are committed to continuously improving as a leader.

It isn't always easy to admit our shortcomings, especially if the desired result was achieved, but in most cases, there are at least one or two things we could have done better. I like to use a sports analogy to illustrate the point: even the greatest athletes have coaches and continue to practice even after they win because they always want to get better.

If you're not accustomed to self-reflection, start with a simple question about a specific situation: *Did I treat others as I want to be treated (Golden Rule)?*

If the answer is yes, which of the CARE Leadership Tools were most effective, and which ones could you have applied better?

If the answer is no, dig deeper: *Why didn't I? What am I going to do next time to make sure I do treat others how I want to be treated using the CARE Leadership Tools?*

Simple, as promised.

Being self-critical isn't always easy and might not come naturally to some people. That's why I've included several case studies to detail failures and successes. My intention is to show examples of people being self-critical and applying the CARE Leadership Tools to real-life situations.

This is a great way to practice being self-critical, but

I believe the best way is to think about how the CARE Leadership Tools might have been applied to your past experiences. Reflecting on your own experiences will allow you to practice being self-critical and become more familiar with applying the CARE Leadership Tools naturally in your day-to-day activities. In fact, when I teach the CARE Leadership Tools, one of the activities the students are asked to do is identify some experiences from their lives and apply the CARE Leadership Tools.

The Tools Explained

The CARE Leadership Tools don't need a lot of elaboration. I will list the key elements that my experiences have shown are essential to being a successful leader. As you read through each of the CARE Leadership Tools and the real-life experiences that follow, remember the Golden Rule. Ask yourself: "How would I want to be treated?"

Communication

1. Without clear and consistent communication, people will make up rumors. In many cases, it'll take more work to dispel those rumors than it would have to communicate clearly in the first place. Think about it. Have you ever either believed a rumor or participated in the proliferation of a rumor absent the facts? I think in most cases, if people had the facts, the rumor would not

have spread, and the confusion, chaos and lack of trust could have been avoided.

2. As leaders, if we don't clearly communicate our expectations, standards, and policies, folks will create their own. In the best case, this can result in less-than-desirable performance; in the worst case, it will cause chaos. In addition, it's common sense that we can't expect our employees to work to a standard that has not been clearly communicated. Have you ever been in a scenario where you thought you understood what was expected of you only to find out you really didn't? As a leader, I'm sure you have had moments when you thought to yourself, *I know I said that. I'm sure I sent an email. Why aren't my employees doing what I told them to do?*

At this point, you can either seek to be right and throw your hands up in frustration because you believe you communicated clearly, or you can choose to figure out what else you can do to clearly communicate with your employees. Admittedly, we all like to be right, but sometimes you need to see the bigger picture and determine how you can improve your communication practices to ensure your message is received.

3. Keep communications as transparent and as frequent as possible. This sounds simple, but there are some cases when it might not be so straightforward, especially when it comes to transparency. There will be times when you have a piece of information that employees want to know, but you just can't tell them yet for a variety of reasons. In this case, the best approach is probably to be transparent about not being able to be transparent. In other words, don't deny knowing the information if asked. Confirm that you have some information, promise to

communicate as soon as possible, and then follow up on that promise.

In some cases, your employees might be mad that you won't communicate the whole story, but at least if you are honest with them and promise to follow up with the full story later, they can appreciate the honesty and follow-through, which strengthens relationships.

4. The most-forgotten element of excellent communication is the ability—and, more important, the willingness—to listen. If employees don't feel they are being listened to, building trust is nearly impossible. And without trust, both individual and organizational successes are unlikely. Another quick tie to the Golden Rule.

Think about a time when you were speaking to someone who was clearly not giving you their full attention or was distracted by their surroundings. How did that make you feel? On a personal level, there is nothing more impactful than making your employees feel like they are truly being listened to. In addition, this gives them the confidence to approach you with a concern or an idea when the time comes. I find the best way to do this is to go to a quiet location to minimize distractions and to put my cell phone in a drawer or turn it off to avoid the temptation to look at it.

Once you have eliminated distractions, really focus on what the other person is saying. Don't try to formulate your response while they are still talking. That's thinking, not listening. This isn't easy, but it's important. If anyone has a tried-and-true tool that can help with this, please let me know. You can email me at alecmcgalliard@gmail.com.

Accountability

Contrary to popular belief, accountability is not a four-letter word (obviously, it has fourteen letters). It seems that in today's society, if we say someone needs to be held accountable for something, we are being mean-spirited and are branded a "crotchety old man," as my kids often call me. Since when is it wrong to expect or ask someone to do what they said they were going to do, what they know they are supposed to do, and what they are getting paid to do? That's what accountability is all about.

Here's a quick tie back to the first CARE Leadership Tool—Communication. Effective communication of our expectations, standards, and policies will ensure people know what they are being held accountable for. What follows are the key elements to having an accountable workforce:

1. As a new leader/supervisor/manager, make sure you establish that you will hold folks accountable for their actions or inaction. It is more difficult to establish a culture of accountability after you previously failed to hold people accountable.

2. Methods of holding people accountable come in many forms. This might include performance reviews, coaching/feedback, bonus structure, constructive discipline, and termination. Use whatever methods work best for you and your organization. For example, not all businesses have a bonus plan that is tied to individual or group performance, so a different method of accountability would be necessary. The key is to make sure that everyone understands the accountability model/process that will be used and that you are consistent with its application.

3. Clearly communicate (another tie back to Communication) what system and methods of measurement will be used to determine success or failure. This way no one is surprised when you tell them they didn't meet expectations and are being held accountable as a result.

4. Not holding someone accountable is a detriment to the organization and to the individual. Lack of accountability hurts the organization in many ways. One of the most effective methods of accountability is tying personal performance to financial compensation. If the individual knowingly continues their undesirable behavior, their chances for advancement will be impacted. In addition, if the organization has a bonus structure tied to individual performance—that will be impacted as well.

5. Whatever process or form is being used, ensure that accountability occurs as soon as possible and is very

specific. Think about it: if you were doing something wrong or not up to expectations, wouldn't you want to know as soon as possible? And wouldn't you need to know specifically what you were doing wrong so you could fix it? Of course you would. Treat others like you want to be treated. There it is again—the Golden Rule!

6. Don't forget, accountability applies to your employees, your peers, and to you as a leader. Holding yourself accountable and expecting others to hold you accountable when you don't meet expectations is essential. We need to be accountable to our company's processes by modeling them (more on that in the Example of Excellence discussion). For example, if your company has a policy that limits rental cars to mid-size only, but you routinely rent a full-size car, are you holding yourself accountable for following company policy?

Relationships

Ask yourself this question: If I believed my supervisor/manager/director/executive really cared about me, would I be more or less likely to meet and exceed expectations?

I have worked for people who couldn't care less about me. The only thing that motivated me to meet and exceed expectations was a personal sense of pride and my work ethic.

In contrast, when I was employed by people who had my best interest at heart, I worked my butt off for them. I would like to think that everyone has that same pride and work ethic, but something tells me that is not realistic. In view of this, prioritizing a positive relationship with employees is essential to effective leadership.

A few key takeaways from the importance of relationships:

1. In order to get the level of effort that goes beyond minimum expectations, you need to build caring relationships with your employees. This level of effort is often referred to as discretionary effort and is defined as that which a person could do if he/she wanted to do, but if they didn't do it, nothing bad would happen to them.

2. Don't go overboard on #1. Here is an example. I have heard people claim that their boss took the time to learn the names of their employees' spouses, kids, grandkids, dogs, and so on. More power to those bosses, but for most people, that is not realistic. I like to think of it this way: In order to show a sense of caring, invest in people professionally. Look for opportunities for them to grow into a new position suited to their talents, or to take on a special project. Make sure you put folks in situations where they can be successful.

And with regard to personal lives, make sure you know if someone is celebrating a significant milestone (birth of a child/grandchild, anniversary, birthday, graduation), and celebrate appropriately. In addition, make sure you know if someone is experiencing a personal hardship (personal illness, family illness, death in the family, etc.) and be as flexible as possible should they need time to deal with these situations. One of the life experiences I share later in the book will illustrate the importance of knowing the challenges your employees are facing.

3. Relationships can be fragile, and people have short memories. In our "what have you done for me lately" culture, we need to be aware of how we treat people. We need to treat people with respect and like adults.

Speaking to someone in a demeaning way in a display of power is one of the most damaging things you can do to a relationship. It creates a lasting effect that is difficult to overcome. Again, just think about how you feel when someone speaks to you like you're an incompetent child.

4. Without trust, you have very little chance of forming a good relationship. If you say you are going to do something, do it. In addition, do not discuss your employees' performance or any personal issue they have confided in you with other employees—a clear application of the Golden Rule.

Example of Excellence

As leaders, we must set the example for how we want our folks to conduct themselves—if we want excellence, our behavior must model excellence. I have been reluctant to use quotes from famous people in this book, but the following quote about leaders setting the right example really speaks to me:

"Setting an example is not the main means of influencing others, it is the only means."

—Albert Einstein[1]

1. In terms of leadership, few things are worse than a leader who sets a poor example and is then surprised when his or her expectations, standards, and policies are not met.

---

1 "Albert Einstein quotes," goodreads.com, accessed Dec. 20, 2018, https://www.goodreads.com/quotes/84604-setting-an-example-is-not-the-main-means-of-influencing.

The person who behaves this way lacks credibility, which makes it very difficult to lead. Accountability, one of our previous CARE Leadership Tools, applies here as personal accountability and is crucial at every level of an organization.

2. When a leader is "in the field," as we call it in the nuclear industry, they influence behavior through the example they set. Keep in mind, "the field" is pretty much everywhere if you are a leader; folks are always watching what you're doing, how you're communicating, and how you're handling situations.

3. Excellence should almost always be the goal. The only exception is when you have a detailed business model or research concluding that excellence does not make sense financially, as long as the risk of not being excellent is acceptable.

4. Anyone truly striving for excellence can find something to improve on in almost every task they complete, even if the task was a success.

The ability to reflect on performance and always look for something to improve on, no matter how small, is what separates good from great. This is true at both the professional and personal level.

If you're a sports fan, think about the athletes and teams that win championships: Do they still practice? Of course they do. They always want to be better. And they realize that even when they are successful, they can always improve on their weaknesses.

Part II

Case Studies

As you read through each of the real-life experiences below, think about similar situations in your work environment. How might you have achieved a more positive result by implementing the CARE Leadership Tools and living your life by the Golden Rule? I will provide my humble opinion, highlighting elements of each of the CARE Leadership Tools and how they might have created a better outcome for all involved.

Experience 1

I mentioned earlier being on the receiving end of some pretty crappy leadership. The experience I am about to share happened to me a few years ago. It's the best example I can think of to illustrate that leaders who don't model desired behaviors fail to get desired results from employees—and often damage professional relationships. I need to set the stage a little.

The company I worked for at the time of the event had a clearly understood expectation that we would use the concepts described in the book *Crucial Conversations* by Al Switzler, Joseph Grenny, and Ron McMillan, anytime we were at work. This had been reinforced on multiple occasions by the executive involved in this case. We were expected to model the principles and behaviors associated with *Crucial Conversations* and provide coaching and feedback to those folks who did not.

For the record, I am a strong believer in most of the elements and principles of *Crucial Conversations*—both at work and in my personal life—so I have no issue with modeling those behaviors, and I try to do so even today.

As a division manager with this company, I was required to update the senior executives, including the president of the company, on how things were going in my area of responsibility. In this update, I was to discuss challenges we were facing and mention any help needed (or so I thought). Our senior managers and executives touted this periodic update as an example of how, as an organization and an executive team, we were open to hearing challenges and asking for help. So let's see how well they reinforced this value and set the example.

The executive I reported to required me to brief him prior to the meeting with the executive team. I prepared the required presentation material and went to the executive's office for the pre-meeting. The moment arrived for me to mention challenges and ask for help.

I brought up, as I had on several previous occasions, that we were having trouble filling two positions, which really had us spread thin.

I was concerned that we would be challenged meeting several milestones. At this point, I was expecting the executive to demonstrate *Crucial Conversations* skills to get the facts on the table, understand my perspective, and ask what he could do to help. It didn't turn out that way.

What followed felt like it lasted an hour, though it was probably more like five minutes. The executive's first question following my discussion of challenges and my request for help went something like this:

Executive (leaning forward with an unpleasant look and tone): "Do you like acting?"

Me: Silent, as I scanned my brain for the right answer.

Executive: "Do you like politics?"

Me: Silent, shocked, and stuttering. Eventually

sputtered out "no," which turned out to be the wrong answer.

Executive: "Well, you'd better learn to like it, because you are not going to tell the president of this company about not being able to fill a position and make the rest of us look incompetent."

I was shocked, to say the least. Was this the same guy who had repeatedly said we were to use *Crucial Conversations*? I thought the whole point of having a "challenges and help needed" portion of the conversation was to discuss challenges and help needed! My mistake.

As I left his office, my first thought (well, maybe not my first thought) was that the executive was a hypocrite. Here this guy had been saying one thing about modeling *Crucial Conversations* anytime he was in front of a group of people, yet behind closed doors, he made no effort to actually follow through.

Do you think that helped reinforce the expectation to use *Crucial Conversations*?

Did the meeting with the executives prove to be valuable in identifying areas where help was needed? Clearly, the answer was no—to both questions. The executive did not set a good example of leadership.

Let's use the CARE Leadership Tools of Communication, Accountability, Relationships and Example of Excellence to analyze this experience.

Communication

While sarcasm and rhetorical questions have their place, I contend that in this situation, they were not the method of communication needed to arrive at the stated desired outcome of the meeting. I left the meeting wondering many things, one being, *What are his expectations?*

In addition, how well do you think the executive listened to my concerns?

Accountability

In addition to holding our employees accountable, we have a responsibility to hold ourselves accountable as leaders. This includes being accountable for how we implement and support processes we expect our employees to support. In this case, the executive had zero accountability for his behavior, as he believed he'd done nothing wrong, even though he'd clearly failed to follow the very model he professed to support. What will prevent him from conducting himself in the same way in the future if there is no accountability?

Relationships

Relationships are fragile, and this experience certainly left a lasting negative impression on me. Earlier we discussed the importance of relationships and how they impact a person's willingness to go above and beyond the minimal effort required. How willing do you think I was or anyone else would be to put forth effort beyond minimum compliance for this leader? Was I treated with respect? Did he approach me as an adult? You be the judge.

Example of Excellence

A powerful leader leads by example. It really is as simple as that. A good leader will model the behavior he or she wishes to see in employees. When leaders' words and actions don't match, they lose credibility.

Let's imagine the same scene from above, this time using the CARE Leadership Tools. After discussing my challenges/help needed with the executive, the conversation could have gone like this:

Executive: "Have you discussed this with the Human Resources Department to let them know how important it is to fill these positions?

Me: "Yes, but we still haven't made any progress."

Executive: "Let's work with Human Resources to develop a plan to help resolve the issue before taking this to the rest of the Executive Team."

Me: "That sounds great! I will set up a meeting in the next couple days. Thanks for your support!"

Experience 2

Experience 1 illustrates what it's like to be on the receiving end of poor leadership. This next example illustrates a time when I provided poor leadership. I believe that looking back at our failures as well as our successes is essential if we want to improve as leaders and as human beings. In the nuclear industry, we call that *using operating experience* or *lessons learned*, and it's a key element in the cycle of continuous improvement. In addition, this aligns with the CARE Leadership Tool of Accountability, as we are all responsible for our performance and for taking steps to improve.

In my twenty-seven-plus years in the commercial nuclear industry, the event that I am least proud of is my role in driving one of my best employees to leave work one day to "go home and check on some contractors" and never return to work—not even to process out through Human Resources. Admittedly, this employee was eligible for retirement, but he'd planned to work at least one more year.

This gentleman is one of the finest people you will ever meet, and he had a very respectable career spanning many years.

He served as sort of an unofficial mentor to me in my first position as a manager, and for that I will always be grateful.

Our small work group had recently experienced some attrition (a retirement and two unexpected internal postings to other positions in the company), so we were operating with two fewer people than usual. This resulted in an increased workload for the remaining people in the department. Because this gentleman was a very hard worker, I relied on him during this tough time, and he picked up more work than anyone else in my department.

In addition, anytime I was away from work, he served

as the acting manager, which piled more onto his already overwhelming workload. He had spent a couple of weeks working with all departments at the company to develop an integrated schedule of the self-assessments we would perform the following year.

This process was very time-consuming and often very frustrating, as many schedules had to be considered. In addition, I asked him to cover a business trip for me to another facility, as I had a conflict. I knew he really didn't want to go, but he accepted the assignment, as usual.

He was very stressed out over the business trip, the development of the self-assessment schedule, and the work of the two vacant positions. I knew it, but I did nothing about it. I did not adequately advocate with my boss or speak to Human Resources about expediting filling the two vacant positions, and I did a poor job distributing the workload among the other folks in our group. In other words, I didn't listen to my best employee, was not accountable for my own actions, didn't guard our relationship, and failed to set a good example. Besides that, I did everything right.

The situation came to a head when, after this employee had worked tirelessly on the self-assessment schedule, we had a meeting with the key stakeholders to discuss and agree on the schedule.

One of our executives came to the meeting—which he rarely did—and shot down the whole schedule, not knowing the effort that had gone into its development. He dictated which self-assessments we were to do and walked out of the room.

As the executive spoke, my best employee's face turned pale then beet red.

What did I do as his leader? Nothing! I just sat there. I did nothing to advocate for my employee and the effort he had put into the project. As soon as the meeting ended, my employee asked if he could run home for a few minutes to check on some contractors at his house, and I have not seen him since. That was over seven years ago.

I blame myself for this man feeling so desperate that he had no other choice but to quit an employer he'd worked for over twenty years.

Had I only done a better job of listening to my top performer, perhaps I could have avoided this situation and not driven him to quit in such a drastic fashion.

In contrast to Experience 1, Experience 2 is about my failure to apply the CARE Leadership Tools to my own performance as described below.

Communication

This instance was another example of poor listening. I did not listen to my employee and therefore was not aware of how frustrated he truly was.

Accountability

The most disturbing part about this case is that it took writing this book for me to really hold myself account-able for my role in losing this employee.

Relationships

Earlier in this book I talked about the importance of relationships and how a strong relationship can help motivate employees to put forth that extra effort. In this case, not only did I fail in relationship building, I drove an employee to quit.

Example of Excellence

The executive and I set a poor example for the people in the room and in the department that day. Our actions suggested we didn't really need to follow the established process, even though as leaders we constantly communicated that expectation to our employees. Another very poor example of modeling desired behaviors.

As a footnote to this experience, I never spoke to or heard from the employee again. I think he moved away following his sudden retirement, and I never had the courage to reach out to him—another regret on my part.

Experience 3

My first real experience—you might even say test—in holding one of my employees accountable for their behavior came soon after I was promoted to a supervisory role in our engineering department. My engineering section staff consisted of a group of very experienced and seasoned engineers. Everyone in the department had more experience in engineering than I had. An older gentleman I had previously worked with, when I was a student and he was an instructor, was in the department as well.

I had and still have great admiration for this man, who has a great sense of humor and is a very fun person to work with. I have never known anyone who didn't like working with this guy.

On this particular day, he and I were attending a meeting about one of his programs that involved several members of another department. The program had fallen behind industry standards before he took over as the new program owner, and he'd had a frustrating time getting support to drive the needed improvements.

As the meeting progressed, the tone in the room became very contentious and heated at times.

As the meeting continued to degrade, the employee used some unprofessional language and stormed out of the room, refusing to work with the folks in the room. As the meeting ended and I began the ten-minute walk back to my office, I realized that, as a leader, I could not let that behavior go unchecked.

When I arrived at my office, I solicited feedback from one of the other engineering supervisors, and we agreed to implement the constructive discipline program for this individual's behavior.

This was not an easy decision for me. As I stated earlier, I had tremendous respect for this person and actually agreed with some of the things he'd said in the meeting—just not the way he'd said it.

I called this man to my office and proceeded to document the event in accordance with our constructive discipline program. I could see he was shocked that I would choose to go this route. After I finished speaking, he stood up and told me that, in his thirty-plus years in the nuclear industry, he had never had anything negative placed in his personnel file.

As we finished the session and he left my office, I was rather saddened, as I feared I had permanently damaged a relationship that I truly valued.

To my surprise, not a half hour went by before he reappeared and thanked me for letting him know that his behavior was not acceptable. You could have knocked me over with a feather. Despite my concerns, that event made our relationship stronger than it had ever been.

Communication

One of the keys to making the above interaction a

success is that the employee was well aware of the expectations and standards for conduct. As a result, he wasn't surprised when his behavior was compared to expectations.

Accountability

This is a great example of Accountability. As a new leader/supervisor/manager, make sure you establish early on that you will hold folks accountable for their actions or inaction. It is more difficult to establish a culture of accountability if you previously or initially failed to hold people accountable.

Relationships

This shows how treating a person with respect while holding them accountable for their behavior can strengthen a relationship. In addition, the relationship we'd built prior to this event helped this awkward situation result in a more positive outcome.

Example of Excellence

During the conversation, we used the *Crucial Conversations skills*, which was the expectation at our place of employment. By modeling these skills, I set the right example for the employee and reinforced the expectation for their use.

Experience 4

Earlier I shared a negative experience I had with an executive in our company. As I look back on the events of that day, I'm reminded of the kind of leader I do not want to be. In my humble opinion, that event was one of the worst examples of leading by example that I have ever seen. Ironically, one of the best examples of leadership involved the same executive. This just proves the point that we all have bad days.

The example of great leadership that I am about to share is a very personal story.

My wife was diagnosed with breast cancer in February 2011. The treatment plan outlined for us included multiple surgeries, chemotherapy, and radiation treatments at a hospital about an hour and a half away. Before I go any further with this, I'll put you at ease—my wife is now cancer-free. We are very fortunate to have a world-renowned cancer hospital so close to us and a great employee insurance plan that supported us through her treatment.

When I found out all the details of the treatment, I let the executive, know what was going on. A couple days after we talked, he asked me to come to his office to discuss some things. Based on the previous experience that I'd shared with this person, to say I was a little worried would be an understatement.

But as I sat in his office, he explained that he and the rest of the executive team had made a decision. Given the level of involvement I would need to have in my wife's treatment and the care of our two children—and the fact that my current management position was very demanding—they'd decided to take me out of that role and place me in a "special project" role until my wife recovered.

This new role would allow me more flexibility and would not result in reduced compensation. I remember how relieved I felt when he told me the news. I hadn't had the courage to ask to be removed from my position so I could focus on my family. And trying to do both would likely have kept me from doing either job well.

The executive told me he understood how important family is and that one day I might have an opportunity to "pay it forward." To this day, I consider this one of the best things anyone has ever done for me and my family. I will always be grateful for their decision.

I believe this is what leadership is all about—fostering relationships and leading by example.

Communication

The executives listened to my situation and understood the impact on my family and my job. This allowed them to make a decision that was best for me and the company.

Accountability

The executives and senior leaders understood their role

in the company. They recognized the demands on my time could impact my performance and negatively affect company performance. As a result, they took responsibility for making the required change. They knew holding me accountable for the actions associated with a very demanding position was not fair or realistic given the situation.

Relationships

After my wife's treatments were complete, I had a renewed sense of loyalty and dedication to the leadership team that clearly had my best interest at heart. This renewed commitment resulted in my being a better employee and leader.

Becoming aware of personal hardship (personal illness, family illness, death in the family, etc.) and being as flexible as possible goes a long way toward building and strengthening relationships.

Example of Excellence

The executives demonstrated the right behaviors. They laid the groundwork for me to "pay it forward" should I ever be in a similar situation as a leader.

Experience 5

I hold the person in this story in very high regard, in part because of this experience, which so perfectly illustrates Example of Excellence.

The company I work for hired a new president and chief executive officer a few years ago. He was brought in, in part, to improve our profitability in the very competitive electrical generation market in Texas. I know what you're thinking: "improve profitability" is secret code for layoffs and cutting expenses. Well, you are partially correct. While we did not have any layoffs, we did find ways to cut unnecessary expenses, which in some cases were not very popular.

The point of this real-life experience is how our president and CEO modeled the desired behavior. First, we instituted a "carry out your own trash" policy, meaning each employee was responsible for emptying their own office/cubicle trash can, and our CEO was right there with us. Does your CEO take out his/her own trash? Second, we were asked to give up our individual printers in an effort to save on printer supplies. Again, our CEO gave up his printer.

Finally, I witnessed firsthand how our CEO reduced travel expenses. He and I were traveling to Washington, DC, for a monthly industry meeting. Prior to his arrival, I had traveled with one of our other executives. In those early days, we often took commercial flights that cost over $1,000, stayed in hotels that cost over $500 a night, and took a private car to the hotel from the airport. The first time I traveled to Washington, DC, after our new CEO arrived, I noticed he wasn't on my flight and wasn't staying at my hotel. We started discussing travel habits, and I realized how frivolous I had been.

My new CEO took cheaper flights, which in many cases involved a layover and a later arrival in Washington, DC. He also stayed at cheaper hotels and used the DC Metro system. Talk about setting the right example—wow!

Communication

Most leaders know that any messaging around "reducing cost" must be clear and concise. It must clearly explain why the reductions are necessary and how they will be beneficial. We also know that even when the communications meet this standard, there will still be naysayers. Our new CEO did a great job of communicating the need for cost reductions and demonstrated how we were reinvesting the savings back into the company. In addition, when he discussed my frivolous travel habits with me, he calmly and clearly stated how I could be a better steward of the company's money.

Accountability

When he held me accountable for my travel budget, it forced me to look at more frugal methods of travel. This benefited both the company and my own family, as I also changed my recreational travel habits.

Relationships

I previously mentioned how calm and non-accusing my CEO was when he first discovered my travel habits. I have seen these types of conversations conducted in a demeaning manner, which almost always damages relationships. I feel very fortunate to have a personal relationship with my CEO (though he is now retired and living in Florida), and I look back on this early interaction as the foundation for our strong relationship.

Example of Excellence

The CEO's positive handling of this situation set a perfect example of how I'd want to approach an employee were I in a similar circumstance.

The examples above are real-life experiences. I hope as you reflect on these, you'll think about what went well and what could have been improved with the help of the CARE Leadership Tools. I am guessing that most people reading this book can relate to these situations. If not, perhaps you can use the CARE Leadership Tools to avoid the mistakes you've read about.

Afterword
The Traditional Meaning of Care

In the Introduction, I stated that if you don't care about your performance, your job, your coworkers, or your employees, you need to seriously consider changing jobs. That may sound preachy—I don't mean it to come across that way. I do believe, though, that caring about all aspects of your job, including the folks you work with, results in a more rewarding professional experience and provides for a more stress-free personal life.

Again, this is common sense, as I believe most people who get up every day and look forward to going to work are happier at work and at home.

As promised: short, sweet, and to the point. The CARE Leadership Tools don't require a certification—just common sense. These tools are based on personal experience from someone who started at the bottom, has worked his way up to management, has aspirations for further career advancement, and is just trying to be a better leader one day at a time.

I really believe the CARE Leadership Tools will work for you and will help you avoid some of the mistakes I've made or been on the receiving end of. Being a good leader—much less a great leader—is not easy. I hope to be a great leader one day.

Appendix
Implementation Tool

The following is a five-step implementation tool I hope will serve as a blueprint for how to begin using the CARE Leadership Tools.

1. Read the entire book and apply the CARE Leadership Tools to your own experiences.

2. Look at the CARE Leadership Tools as common sense. You don't need a certification or extensive research to understand and apply the tools. Personal experience shows these are powerful tools for effective leadership.

3. If you see a leadership challenge on the horizon, refer back to the CARE Leadership Tools to try to prepare as much as possible.

4. If you have recently experienced a leadership

challenge, reflect on the challenge and see how you might have minimized, simplified, or possibly avoided the challenge by implementing the CARE Leadership Tools.

5. If this stuff works for you, share it with your peers, friends, and family.

Acknowledgments

I would like to recognize a few folks who helped me in the early stages of writing this book.

My son, Grant, an outstanding sports journalist, provided the first proofread for grammar, spelling, and punctuation. This saved me from embarrassment when I showed it to anyone else.

Lisa Clark, a fantastic leadership development training instructor and someone who doesn't mince words, was the first person to read the book, and she gave me valuable insights for content.

Finally, Tim Rausch—recognized across the nuclear industry as an outstanding leader—provided additional insights. I greatly appreciated his feedback.

Thanks to all of you for taking the time to help me through this process.

Finally, I'd like to thank my family: Carrie, my wife of

twenty-four-plus years, and my two kids, Grant and Chloe. They keep me grounded, laugh at my ranting and raving about a variety of things, and inspire me to be better every day. I realize that being inspired by your family is probably a cliché, but I think I already mentioned that I am a very simple, normal person.

My late father, Larry McGalliard, taught me the value of hard work at an early age and set a great example for me of how to be a good person.

Last, but certainly not least, I thank my Nana. The late Kathleen Clarke McGalliard remains one of the most inspirational and influential people in my life. Nana was born and raised in the mountains of North Carolina, had an eighth-grade education, and is to this day one of the most insightful people I have ever met. She had many colloquial sayings and pieces of advice that stuck with me over the years, but the one thing she always insisted on was following the Golden Rule.

Thank You for Reading

Thank you so much for choosing to be on this journey to becoming a better leader with me. I am glad that you stopped by.

Visit my website mcgalliardconsulting.com to learn more about how we can work with your organization to continue the development of your company's leaders.

Please do not hesitate to connect with me if you have any questions about this book, or if you just want someone to chat with.

I would be happy to hear from you and I enjoy connecting with readers.

Thanks again,

-Alec McGalliard

A Quick Favor Please?

A quick favor before you go. Would you please leave this book a review on Amazon?

Reviews are very important and help authors like me to share our services so we can help more people and influence better leaders for tomorrow.

Please take a quick minute to go to Amazon and leave this book an honest review. I promise it doesn't take long, but it can help this book reach more readers just like you.

Thank you so much reading and for being part of the journey of writing my first book!

-Alec McGalliard

About the Author

Alexander (Alec) C. McGalliard was born and raised in Lenoir, North Carolina. He served six years in the United States Navy Nuclear Submarine Force as a nuclear mechanical operator (Machinist Mate). After his service in the US Navy, he began his twenty-seven-year career in the commercial nuclear power industry, where he continues to serve today. He has a background in organizational effectiveness, continuous improvement, operations, engineering, corporate communications, and project management.

Mr. McGalliard has a Master of Science degree in Management and a Bachelor of Science degree in Nuclear Engineering Technology. He continues on his journey to be a great leader. Alec is the founder, owner, and CEO of McGalliard Consulting (LLC).